D1608675

BUILDING SITE ENSCHEDE
A city re-creates itself

Theo Baart
Ton Schaap

NAi Publishers

Colofon

Building Site Enschede is an initiative of Theo Baart and Ton Schaap and is published in collaboration with NAi Publishers.

This publication was made possible, in part, by the Gemeente Enschede, Jeroen Hatenboer and Jan Jansen.

Concept and compilation Theo Baart, Ton Schaap
Photography Theo Baart
Text and plan selection Ton Schaap
Copy editing D'laine Camp
Translation Pierre Bouvier
Design Axis Media-ontwerpers, Eric van der Wal
Lithography Colorset, Amsterdam
Printing and binding Drukkerij Roelofs, Enschede
Paper 170 grs Hello Silk
Production Alma Timmer
Project coordinator Brecht Bleeker, NAi Publishers
Publisher Eelco van Welie, NAi Publishers

With thanks to Remy Korsman and Tom Kamphuis

Illustration credits Gemeente Enschede page 2, 3, 8, 9, 10, 11, 12 en 102; AVIODROME Luchtfotografie – Lelystad, page 5; Allard van der Hoek, page 64.

It was not possible to find all the copyright holders of the illustrations used. Interested parties are requested to contact NAi Publishers, Mauritsweg 23, 3012 JR Rotterdam, the Netherlands, info@naipublishers.nl

NAi Publishers is an internationally orientated publisher specialized in developing, producing and distributing books on architecture, visual arts and related disciplines.
www.naipublishers.nl

Available in North, South and Central America through D.A.P./Distributed Art Publishers Inc, 155 Sixth Avenue 2nd Floor, New York, NY 10013-1507, tel +1 212 627 1999, fax +1 212 627 9484, dap@dapinc.com

Available in the United Kingdom and Ireland through Art Data, 12 Bell Industrial Estate, 50 Cunnington Street, London W4 5HB, tel +44 208 747 1061, fax +44 208 742 2319, orders@artdata.co.uk

Printed and bound in the Netherlands.

ISBN 90-5662-589-4

This Book

The seed for this publication was sown when I ran into the photographer Theo Baart in the lift of the building in which the daily newspaper *De Waarheid* was once published, on the Hoogte Kadijk in Amsterdam. This was in the autumn of 2005. It turned out he had a commission in Enschede's Roombeek, the neighbourhood devastated by the explosion of a fireworks factory in May 2000. I had just completed my first year as a municipal urban planner in Enschede. The city, which he had never visited before, had surprised him. Enschede had turned out to be a modern city set in a landscape as beautiful as a park. In just a few days, the vague image of a dying industrial town, scarred by poverty and vacant factory buildings, had evaporated. Lively, robust and optimistic were now the words of the day.

My fascination with the city dates from my childhood, and during 2005 this was matched by amazement. Until I was 20, Enschede had been the largest city in the Twente region, in the east of the Netherlands. We lived in Almelo and came to Enschede a couple of times a year. The factories there were bigger, the ring boulevard was wider. There were more mysterious footbridges spanning the streets. You could park on the roof of a factory and look out over the huge market square. Under that roof was a labyrinthine shopping centre and the library. There was a broad boulevard lined with chestnut trees, tall buildings and an immense department store, on the opposite side.

Somehow Enschede was also gloomier than Almelo. The old textile industry was in itself not a very cheerful enterprise. They had this in common. Its impending demise hung like a dark cloud over both cities. The collapse had a more devastating effect on Enschede because of the size and dominance of its textile plants.

When I returned in 2005, a section of the boulevard was gone, replaced by a huge, airy square ringed by modern buildings, with the country's largest parking garage underneath. The department store fronted the square as well. Many of the factory buildings had been replaced by residential structures. The city centre had become a paradise of shops and terraces. Behind the wall of the former Schuttersveld textile factory, the gloomiest and most imposing of them all, a furniture centre had been installed. Some things were less attractive than others, but as a whole it exuded an inveterate optimism, an unflinching refusal to give in. The gloom was gone. No one mourned the loss of the textile industry. 'Good riddance to bad rubbish.'

The problem presented by a busy thoroughfare slicing across the city centre had been thoroughly addressed: the centre of the city had become a destination instead of a transit area. The Van Heekplein symbolizes the city as a whole. 'It is a destination, the rail terminus', says poet and writer Willem Wilmink. It is also a point of departure. Enschede is the source of brooks, of membranes, of beer, of car tyres, of an infinitely varied stream of products and of engineering science and know-how. It is no transfer depot or transhipment port. That had always been the case. Thanks to the square, its form was now more suited to its contents.

The drive with which the reconstruction of the devastated Roombeek area was taken on unleashed energy that apparently had never been tapped before. The past is not the defining factor in Enschede. It has not always been prosperous. The future can only be better. Utopia isn't the goal either. Twente people know that Utopia is quite close to Neverland.

From the Outside In

Theo Baart's photographs of the Enschede of today (2006/2007) are joined in this book by plans for the Enschede of tomorrow. The municipal overview of current urban design projects includes 72 plans of varying sorts and sizes. From Number 1, a new plan for Enschede Airport Twente, an area of more than 100 hectares, to Number 72, the integral restructuring of the Lipperkerkstraat. Practically all of the territory of the city is covered by one plan or another. The city is yearning for the future.

A selection of these plans is presented in this book, in a flanking movement from the outside in.

In the first section, trees dominate the picture. Be it the University of Twente or the Vaneker, a new residential neighbourhood of villas in the tree-lined landscape on the northern edge of the city, green is the dominant colour – at least in the aerial photos and often in the photos taken at eye level.

The second section includes plans for the transformation of parts of the city that are or were already built up, a new city within the old city. This is a major category in Enschede. Besides Roombeek there are the converted factory sites, the former railway tracks

and the depots and yards connected to them.

The third section covers the city centre. In relative terms, of all city centres in the Netherlands, the centre of Enschede contains the most jobs and the fewest inhabitants. It also has a unique combination of a small but intact historic core in direct contrast with the scale and the architecture of the second half of the twentieth century. There are high-rises, there is the Van Heekplein, there are parking garages, there are factory buildings with new functions and there are blocks of flats that occupy the former factory sites. The centre is the place that defines the image of a city more than any other. The centre of Enschede has recently expanded and improved substantially. Of all city centres in the Netherlands, it offers the most opportunities for further development. These opportunities are the result of the course of history.

Deceptively Flat

Within the Netherlands, Enschede is comparable to cities such as Tilburg and Eindhoven, and beyond it to Manchester or Lille. These are former industrial areas. They are not situated on major waterways or other transport links. They flourished thanks to the more or less coincidental combination of the

initiative of a few entrepreneurs with an existing urban core. The growth spurt of these cities took place in the nineteenth and twentieth centuries. Enschede's architectural capital also dates from this period, from the garden suburb of Pathmos to the UT campus, from the CityHall by Friedhoff to the synagogue and the villas by De Bazel, Rietveld and Eschauzier. Starting in the mid-twentieth century, its industry began to disappear. What remained were vacant buildings and industrial sites and disused infrastructure, space directly abutting the historic city core, in the middle of a sprawling urban area.

Twente's waters meet in Almelo. The transit roads run past Borne, Hengelo and Oldenzaal. Enschede is a city on a hill. This is subtly manifested by a constant rise and fall of the ground surface. You can see this when you look closely at the photographs. You can feel it when you're cycling. Topographic maps show that elevations vary from 24 m above NAP (Normal Amsterdam Level) on the Hengelo side to 38 m above NAP on the German border at Glanerburg. By then you've already passed the highest point, 65 m above sea level near Lonneker. From the easternmost to the westernmost bend of the ring, a distance of more than 2 km, the elevation differen-

tial is about 15 m. In and around the Blijdensteinpark, the side of the retaining wall upon which the city lies is visible, once you know that the rolling lawns form part of a great wave in the ground. Its crest lies east of the park, concealed under houses and gardens.

Nowhere is there a dramatic perspective that forever fixes the location in the mind's eye. The hilly topography is perceptible in the environs of the Usseleres. An *es* is farmland that has acquired a rounded shape through millennia of circular ploughing. *Essen* are among the oldest evidence of human habitation in Twente, akin to the dolmens in Drenthe. Aside from the slight curvature that characterizes every *es*, the openness that also typifies an *es* reveals the presence of other variations in elevation. If some of the vegetation around the Westerval above the Auke Vleerweg were to vanish, and if more buildings in the city centre were to rise above the tree line, you could sense it. A city on a hill in the distance. Once you know, you can also see it in the railway line. On the western side it runs atop a dike; the ring runs under it. At the station, the railway line touches the sloping surface of the city core, or *stadserf*, and then cuts, sunk in, through the highest part of the retaining wall. There the ring crosses above it.

This ring is a monument to the urban planning vision of a mayor. It is no mere converted moat but the legacy of a decision made in the 1930s. The city was expanding. The mayor anticipated the growth of automobile traffic and the need for better roadways. The city had no money. It zoned a ring 29 m wide and 9 km long as a future ring boulevard and imposed a building moratorium on it. Sometime in the 1950s, the circle was closed with the opening of the Edo Bergsma Bridge, named after the initiator. The Bergsma Bridge replaced the viaduct over the Zuiderspoorlijn ('southern railway'), bombarded by accident during the Second World War and immortalized in the schoolroom picture 'Zicht op een industriestad' ('View of an industrial town') with its factory chimneys. The Zuiderspoorlijn is now the Zuiderval, the bridge has been replaced by a level crossing. With double rows of trees, a green central reservation and numerous stately buildings, the ring has become a characteristic element in the city. In one fell swoop, all the radiating roadways, residential areas and industrial complexes were combined into a single entity.

The omnipresent trees, the slope of the retaining wall and the ring are the binding elements in Enschede.

A Department Store in the Woods

'There are trees in every picture', reported the photographer when he was halfway through. I had noticed it too. Enschede is a city in a park. And there are parks in the city. The Volkspark was specially designed for the healthful recreation of workers. History relates that the factory director was in the habit of sharing an alcohol-free beer with his employees on Sundays. Other parks began their existence in more exclusive fashion, as an Arcadian décor for the residents of a villa. Copses, wooded embankments and solitary trees were incorporated into the expansion of the city during the twentieth century.

Despite their abundance, the cutting down of a tree leads to commotion, even though it is sometimes unavoidable. There are plenty to spare, I'd say. The city should simply institute a 'seniority rule'. For any 100-year-old tree to be cut down, at least ten 10-year-old trees should be planted somewhere within the city limits. This would preserve the green character of the city while avoiding total stagnation. The city is now compelled to think about large-scale planting, avenues, boulevards, parks instead of little slivers of greenery. In the Vaneker there is plenty of room for large numbers of new

trees. Along the new bus lanes or the Auke Vleerweg too. Lindens, oaks, beeches, chestnuts or birches.

Coming from Hengelo you cycle through avenues and alleyways to the Enschede ring, via the Drienerloo estate, the Ledeboerpark and the Van Heekpark. From the east the greenery reaches inside the ring with the Wooldrikspark and the Blijdensteinpark – names of factory-owning families. Qualities of great price for a city, in every sense of the term. Most inhabitants of Enschede also have a garden. Of all cities in the Netherlands of comparable or greater size, Enschede has the lowest percentage of apartments. The suburbs include categories familiar throughout the Netherlands, the modernist quarters, from Mekkelholt to the Wesselerbrink, the cabbage-patch parcel allotments of the 1970s and the postmodernism that followed, culminating with Sjoerd Soeters's little neighbourhood in the Eschmarke. They share one common characteristic: each and every one is more spacious and greener than their parallels in other cities. Gradually, a dream of the labour movement became reality: decent, healthy housing made accessible to all. Kitchen gardens became ornamental gardens, labourers became housing consumers. Enschede is a cradle of the Dutch trade

union movement. The priest Alfons Ariëns was one of the initiators of the Catholic trade union. His statue stands on the Ariënsplein, a car park in the middle of the city. The factory owners took greater care with their memorials.

Near the city centre, a concentration of apartments has emerged, as conditions there are unusually favourable. Living on the Blijdensteinpark, within walking distance of the Bijenkorf department store. A green horizon is always visible above the fourth storey, although this depends a bit on the position of the building. Above the fourth storey, Enschede is a clearing in the woods.

Trees in Twente grow to a height of 30 m. Yet few buildings in Enschede are any higher. The leaner and lighter the architecture, the more attractive the contrast with lush vegetation. Le Corbusier outlined this years ago. The closer the trees, the greater the need for light and a view. Big windows, a roof garden: for inventive designers there is never a shortage of options. The university and the aforementioned Blijdensteinpark are examples of what can be done.

There is one downside to the presence of all those trees: a lack of perspective. Sightlines of more than 1 km are rare. There is no panoramic view of the city, like that of Rotterdam

from the Brienenoord Bridge, or of Dordrecht from the river. The city conceals itself. When you drive into Enschede, you think, are we there already? – certainly if your route runs via the Westerval. This route ends at the rear of a small service building in the Volkspark. There is no landmark, no monumental archway or wide vista into the park. You've driven through several kilometres of city and are virtually in the centre. The skyline formed by high-rises now under construction or being planned on the drawing board will change all that. The city will become visible from afar.

Hidden Treasures
The skyline signifies the inversion of another characteristic. Enschede harbours hidden treasures; Enschede is a hidden treasure. The Rijksmuseum Twente is the metaphor for Enschede as a whole. The museum is not striking for the building that houses it, nor for its location. It stands on the ring, and you can easily miss it. Its value lies in its collection, much of which was donated by Twente collectors. To be found by connoisseurs who can appreciate it.
The villas by De Bazel, Rietveld or Eschauzier are not easy to find. And even then you can't get near them, much less inside.

They are encircled by large gardens. The residence and office of Paul van der Jeugd does give directly onto the street; suddenly you find yourself in front of it, a needle in a haystack.
As to the value of the UT complex, even its owners seem scarcely aware of it. 'High-tech in the bush', remarked an American recently. A gradual transformation into a standard-issue industrial estate is looming. The first car parks have already been laid down.
Friedhoff's City Hall is one of the most beautiful in the Netherlands. Some treasures are a bit dusty, like the interior of the City Hall or the Klokkenplas, an unexpectedly intimate open space in the middle of the city, with gorgeous trees. An undiscovered oasis, right behind the City Hall. The Klokken-plas will not escape refurbishment.
The space to build all sorts of things right next to the city centre is an exceptional opportunity. Enschede is a centre for 1,000,000 people, 600,000 in Twente and 400,000 on the German side of the border. You have Münster and Arnhem for a visit every few months. Cologne or Amsterdam once a year. In between Enschede has to do, based on its location and size. There is simply no alternative. If you want to go downtown, or

live a bit more anonymously, if you want to go to the theatre, to the opera, the café, a major bookstore or the biggest gay sauna between Amsterdam and Berlin, there is only one place: Enschede.

Oude Markt
The Oude Markt is beautiful. Nowhere else have I seen a market square of this size that was so completely not intimidating, so 'informal' or 'inviting', if you will. People cut across it without a second thought, instead of proceeding cautiously along the edges. This might have something to do with the lush linden trees, with the shape of the space, which cannot be glimpsed in one overall view, or with the position of the church, which occupies its centre like a kind of cuddly elephant. Nowhere does a square merge so seemingly casually with the adjacent streets. The Dutch word *stadserf*, essentially 'city yard', is well chosen.
Like all village squares in north-western Europe, it exudes a democratic spirit, one of equality among those who reside around it. A self-assured spirit: every building stands with a broad, clearly recognizable façade on the square. No design, no pretension other than to create space, for a market, for a

Enschede, Langestraat

churchyard probably, for the rounding up of cattle, once, in the beginning. Practical considerations would have played a significant role. Respect for the collective domain is nevertheless palpable, even now that it has become a public area, open to everyone who knows how to behave a little.

The double ring of narrow streets that surround the jovial grandeur of the Oude Markt are of a different order entirely. Their origin probably lies in protection against an environment that had apparently become hostile. The bundling of the paths and roadways converging on the city from all sides through two gates is one result. One gate to the west, on the 'open country side', and one to the east, on the 'es side'. These self-imposed boundaries left room only for narrow streets and small properties. The land outside the city walls was set aside for gardens and small fields (*gaarden* in old-fashioned Dutch). This is where the first factories would later rise. This is where the new Muziekkwartier is now being built.

To me the Oude Markt represents an ideal of urban design in a democratic context. It would be nice if the expansions of the city centre exuded the same spirit. They're working on that. One example can already be seen in Roombeek, where the look of the big lawn, the *bleek* (an old Dutch word for a village

green where linen would be laid out to bleach), ringed by houses built for private clients, displays a comparable balance between individual and collective identity.

Time

Books of old picture postcards create the impression that everything used to be prettier. This is probably one reason why the genre is so popular. Streets with simple lines. Pedestrians who stare back at the photographer, cyclists in the middle of the roadway and few, albeit beautiful, cars. Big trees. Everything in black-and-white. This produces a harmonious picture, and the fact that it's about the past is reassuring. The past may not have been ideal, but at least it is fathomable – no surprises. According to some, there is great demand for urban designs that already look like an old postcard upon completion. Complete with elements referring to the past. The fact that the streets are packed with parked cars and that the details, on closer examination, are nothing more than allusions to the original, is accepted as part of the bargain. So long as the illusion is there.

The opposite are the photos of early modern architecture with the same antique cars in front. The optimism with which the

architect embraced the new technological possibilities seems to have defied time. Eternal youth for the Villa Garche, designed by Le Corbusier and built in 1927. The car in a photograph taken at the time looks like a real old-timer. The house would still be considered modern today.

The fact that the avant-garde of international architecture is now predominantly active in Asia and the Middle East seems to me a bad omen for old Europe. A city that closes itself off from the future ceases, in a way, to exist. In Enschede the best collection of eternally young buildings can be found on the campus of the University of Twente. Some of the buildings there are so insouciantly optimistic, robust and straightforward that they age only in a technical sense.

In a genuine city there is room for both of these phenomena. There is a demand for the reassuring effect of architecture that suggests stability by referring to a bygone era. The commercial impact of this is too significant to ignore. Commercial innovations are innovations too.

The tingling sensation of something entirely new, the menthol effect of more air and vistas onto unexpected possibilities give cities magic, appeal. The effect is significant and relatively long-lasting, and indeed it takes a great deal of effort to

realize. Nostalgia can seduce the housing consumer. The tingling inspires new generations and leads to the innovations the building industry needs.

There are plenty of items for the innovation agenda. Energy conservation while maintaining fresh air and ample daylight indoors. Customizing. Better workmanship linked to increased labour wages and better working conditions for construction workers. The use of solar heating and geothermal energy, city-wide, per neighbourhood or per house. Denser construction while maintaining usable exterior space with privacy, comfort and greenery. More comfortable, more frequent, more comprehensive public transport. Buffering of rainwater. Urban housing in apartments and in freehold street-level properties. Innovations will take place in all these areas in coming years, through new inventions and the intelligent combination of recent inventions. The substantive innovations will lead to new forms. In Enschede or elsewhere.

City on a Hill, Enschede in 2030

Barring unforeseen catastrophes, the greater part of Enschede will be completed by 2030. I won't go into the countless conversions, dormer windows, new kitchens, bay windows, gardens and garden houses that will turn Enschede into a building site for the next quarter-century. What will be markedly different in the city in 2030?

From the entrances to the city, the city centre draws attention with a high concentration of high-rises. Enschede has a skyline. A modern version of San Gimignano. Towers on a hill in the distance.

The plans for high-rises near the city centre were eventually all realized. They have been erected with the robustness and the optimism with which the factories were built. They stand alongside surprisingly cosmopolitan buildings in the *stadserf*. The *stadserf* is a succession of streets, alleys, squares and small city parks. It runs from the Molenstraat to the Wooldrik-weg. The scale of the house is never far off and neither are large or tall buildings.

To arrive in the centre is to be engulfed in a bustle of activity, the most important attraction of any city centre. Shops along shopping streets, terraces on squares and green oases under the trees. Back alleys with bars and sleazy cafés like those that exist today merge seamlessly with streets of galleries, jazz clubs and boutiques, the 'one of a kind' type.

The construction of several thousand apartments proved a welcome addition to Twente's quarter-million respectable single-family houses with gardens. Those who want city living or a view of the horizon can move to Enschede. But it's not only apartments that have been added. The University of Twente and the Polytechnic established their academic buildings right next to the place where students can already be found outside lecture hours.

Along with high and low entertainment, culture has landed in the heart of Twente. The galleries, the new library, the film houses, the Vestzak Theatre, the Tor. The Muziekkwartier has been in use for two decades. Spectacular home-grown productions and guests from all over the world.

The Academy for Art and Industry, the AKI, has been operating in the former TETEM factory building for two decades. The new élan attracted new talent, which found its way to the affordable studio spaces in the city. Art and industry rediscovered each other, with a stream of innovations and attractive products as a result.

The statues by Kapoor, Gormley and Eliasson for the Muziekkwartier in 2008 proved to be the start of a statuary garden in the city. The city as statuary park, the statuary park as city. Is this art, is it a cherished or forgotten remnant of a bygone era?

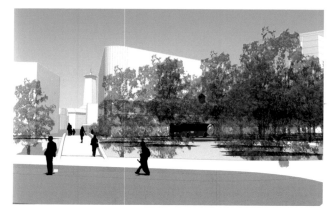  

Did someone put this here yesterday? The Bomarzo gardens are a good inspiration for the urban design of Enschede. Duke Orsini's park in Lazio mocked the self-glorification of his sixteenth-century contemporaries in a theme park *avant la lettre* which is still popular today. Enigmatic, surreal statues in a lovingly designed, somewhat overgrown park.

Gradually the largest collection of statues outside Kröller Müller emerged. What began as a 'culture ribbon' became the exterior collection of the MKMT, the Twente Museum of Modern Art, the successor to the Rijksmuseum Twente. It stretches from the greens of Roombeek to the dusted-off City Hall. The museum has become a new linchpin in the cultural life of the eastern Netherlands. Groundbreaking exhibitions, controversial acquisitions, donations from around the world. The Wilminkgaarde, Klokkenplas, Zuidmolengaarde, Bergsma-plaats and Ledeboerhof have all become little parks. Great trees tower even in the heart of the city. In a series of modern, expansive squares from west to east one can make out the trace of the old Boulevard. The Van Heekplein was there already; the Koningsplein, Diep Gat and Beltplein have been added. High-rises have been erected here. The Diep Gat ('deep hole') links the subterranean world of the Van Heek

garage with the *stadserf*. The northern entrance of the new MST medical centre is connected to the city centre by a bridge over the abyss. Entrance, bridge and City Hall tower turn out to be positioned in a line.

Roombeek, Boddenkamp, Gemeentewerf and Park Schutters-veld have become the most sought-after residential areas of Twente. The timeless luxury of townhouses with small gardens, in peaceful surroundings and within walking distance of the heart of Enschede.

The freight railway line to Lonneker was the foundation for a majestic avenue through Roombeek and Boddenkamp. The bus uses it, the houses stand along it. As though they always had. In the spirit of the Oude Markt. To live here is to have made it. And to have worked hard for it, for most of the houses were built by commission of the residents themselves. The housing consumer is becoming a building citizen.

The UT and the Science Park have merged, connected by the Hengeloosestraat. This has become an avenue. Cars, cyclists and buses ride under double rows of beeches. The park of the Drienerloo estate was restored and expanded. The Roombeek brook flows through it in a serpentine course. The buildings dating from the early days of the University of Twente have

been lovingly restored. They house a continually rejuvenating multitude of inventors and would-be inventors. They excite the curiosity of the students. This promotes the exchange of knowledge and experiences. Successes sort themselves out and establish themselves in the city or around the Twente airport. Or are taken up by companies in need of a new impulse.

Virtually unnoticed, several residential areas have been regen-erated. Carefully, precisely and painstakingly, in close consultation with residents. Inhabitants of the southern and western districts make use of a broad, slightly bulging grass field, 750 x 1000 m, where foot-, cycle and bridle paths make the space almost tangible. Sometimes motocross rallies are held there, or tents are erected for a dance festival. There's always a football match being played somewhere. Mostly it's just used for strolling, cycling or flying kites.

The development of the Twente airport into a new employ-ment area proved successful. New enterprises came. The connections to the rest of Europe brought inspiration and innovation.

This success made it possible to leave the Usseleres un-touched. New avenues of trees were planted along its edges.

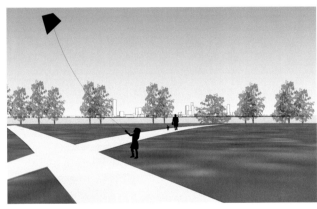

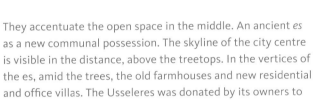

They accentuate the open space in the middle. An ancient *es* as a new communal possession. The skyline of the city centre is visible in the distance, above the treetops. In the vertices of the es, amid the trees, the old farmhouses and new residential and office villas. The Usseleres was donated by its owners to the people of Enschede as a monument to the Twente es.

Building Site Enschede
Making plans is a part of life. Building a house, constructing a street: these are acts of optimism. The implementation of the plan will lead to an improvement of life, in one way or another. That's the idea. This idea provides direction for action, energy and endurance. He who stops making plans is preparing himself for the end. So long as a plan has not been implemented, it can still be changed. This is particularly true of urban designs. They only become reality once the buildings have been designed and built and once the street, the square or the park has been built as well. Urban designs reflect the forces and attitudes of a society. Various parties are involved in the implementation of these plans, each with their own objectives. A good urban design serves multiple objectives. Cashing in the value of a piece of land can be coupled with an improvement of the entire environment. Providing a lane reserved for buses can lead to better proportions in the profile of a street or an avenue, can turn a street into an avenue. The need for surface water to better absorb peaks in rainfall can yield surprising qualities, particularly in a city on a hill. The integration of the various briefs is an opportunity for a city that must make the most of its resources. Designing the water, trees, houses and bus lane as one entity – that is the challenge.

This book is nothing more than a double snapshot in time. What does Enschede look like in 2007 and how do Enschede's planners see the future of the city at that same moment? Does this match what the inhabitants of Enschede themselves want? That will be revealed in the reactions to this book. The photographs in this book are not postcards; they don't just show pretty views of the city – but they do show fascinating ones. We hope Enschede's inhabitants and visitors recognize their city in them. Photographs become obsolete the moment they are taken. Pretty or ugly, the older they get, the more nostalgia they will arouse – that's what time does. Plans become obsolete just as quickly, particularly if they are amended or not implemented, a fate sure to befall a number of the plans published in this book. Of longer life expectancy are the plans that are realized and the optimism, the imagination and the resilience they express. They are a testament to the vitality of Enschede, the building site Enschede.

Ton Schaap, january 2007

Among the Trees

Auke Vleerstraat

The largest residential districts are located on the south side of Enschede. The A35 motorway runs west and south of the city. The Auke Vleerweg is a distributor for automobile traffic to and from these destinations. The plan for improving its place in the landscape and its profile has two objectives: a signature profile for the route as a whole, for better orientation, and a staging of the view to and from the roadway. Twekkelo, a quintessential Twente landscape, will remain intact. Here the road serves as a definitive city limit. A broad, green central reservation, standardized characteristics for detailing, lighting and materials, as well as strategic plantings of trees and shrubs will be used to achieve all that.

The intersection of the Auke Vleerweg and the Westerval, the busiest point on the route and one of the most important entrances into the city, will be stripped of concealing greenery. Embankments lined with broom shrubs and a few solitary trees or copses will lend the setting an identity and a vista. Below, in the near future, in the distance, the city's skyline.

UT Science Park Landscape Plan

Van Tijen and Van Embden designed the campus of the Twente Polytechnic, the forerunner of today's university. A utopian fusion of nature and science. The combination of the Drienerloo estate with hypermodern architecture for housing and teaching was intended to become the ideal breeding ground for the innovators of tomorrow.

Under Jan Hoogstad's supervision, the plan shifted from buildings in a park to clusters of buildings in a park. A research and teaching centre and a housing and living centre. These days the majority of students live off campus. In their free time they've discovered the cinemas near the FC Twente stadium and Enschede's city centre. The discussions between the first generation of modernists, to which the designers of the campus belonged, and the second generation, especially Piet Blom, have thus been overtaken by time. Blom's Bastille was intended to inject urban complexity and intimacy. Students now seek this elsewhere. The Bastille is gone. The conviviality machine that was its interior has been replaced by an office landscape inside the same brick shell.

From the start, consistent detailing of the paths, roadways and car parks suffered from the gradual changes in concept and the increasing use of cars. This led to new car parks and a different access layout.

Time for a new, integral vision for the landscape of the UT, as pictured here. A more prominent role for the water, strict maintenance of the green character through enclosed parking structures and clear guidelines for the style of the park – romantic – and that of the architecture – modern – are just a few of its features.

A set of standard details would restore order in the public areas and do justice to the whimsical nature of the park. That will be the next phase.

Vaneker, Housing in the Landscape

Vaneker is a rolling, typical Twente 'coulisse' landscape on the northern edge of the city. Housing and horse paddocks are, alongside some remaining agriculture, its current functions. Living in the country remains an ideal for many people. By adding villas and trees, a new, sustainable form can be found for this area on the fringe of the city. It offers non-residents a park to cycle or stroll through and gives residents the feeling of being lords of the manor, or at least gentlemen farmers. In order to preserve the essence of the 'park' concept, the illusion of an infinite landscape, in spite of the addition of 150 villas, Twente farmsteads, manor-house apartments in large communal gardens and generous planting of trees and hedges have been employed.

Enschede Airport Twente

The Twente airbase began as the Twente airfield, a private initiative prior to the Second World War. Its military function will shortly come to an end; buildings and land will remain. The runways are in good condition. The city of Enschede and Twente entrepreneurs see opportunities for a new privatized existence, combining an industrial estate with a regional airport. Maintenance operations at Schiphol have manifested interest. So have high-tech industries in the eastern part of the country, which use parts from all over the world. This sketch shows how it might turn out.

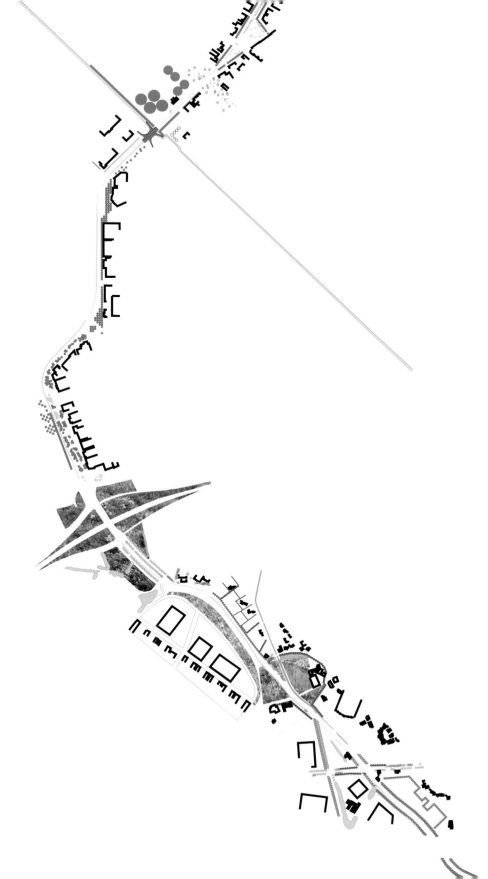

Auke Vleerstraat

___

MTD/DSOB ENSCHEDE
*MTD Niké van Keulen/DSOB Enschede Jaco Kalsbeek,
Erik Rouwette, Kees Lems*

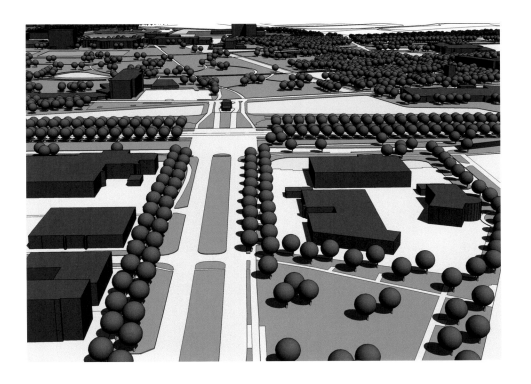

UT Science Park Landscape Plan

LODEWIJK BALJON/DSOB ENSCHEDE
Lodewijk Basljon/DSOB Enschede Markus Götz

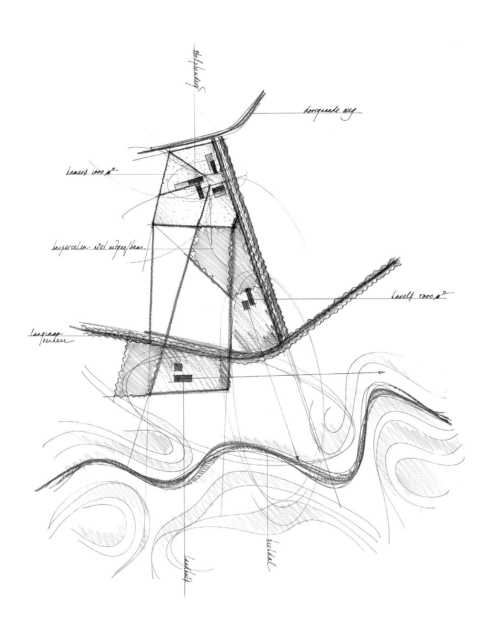

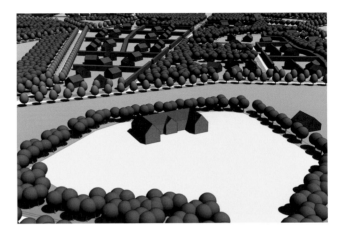

Vaneker, Housing in the Landscape

MTD/DSOB ENSCHEDE
MTD Niké van Keulen/DSOB Markus Götz

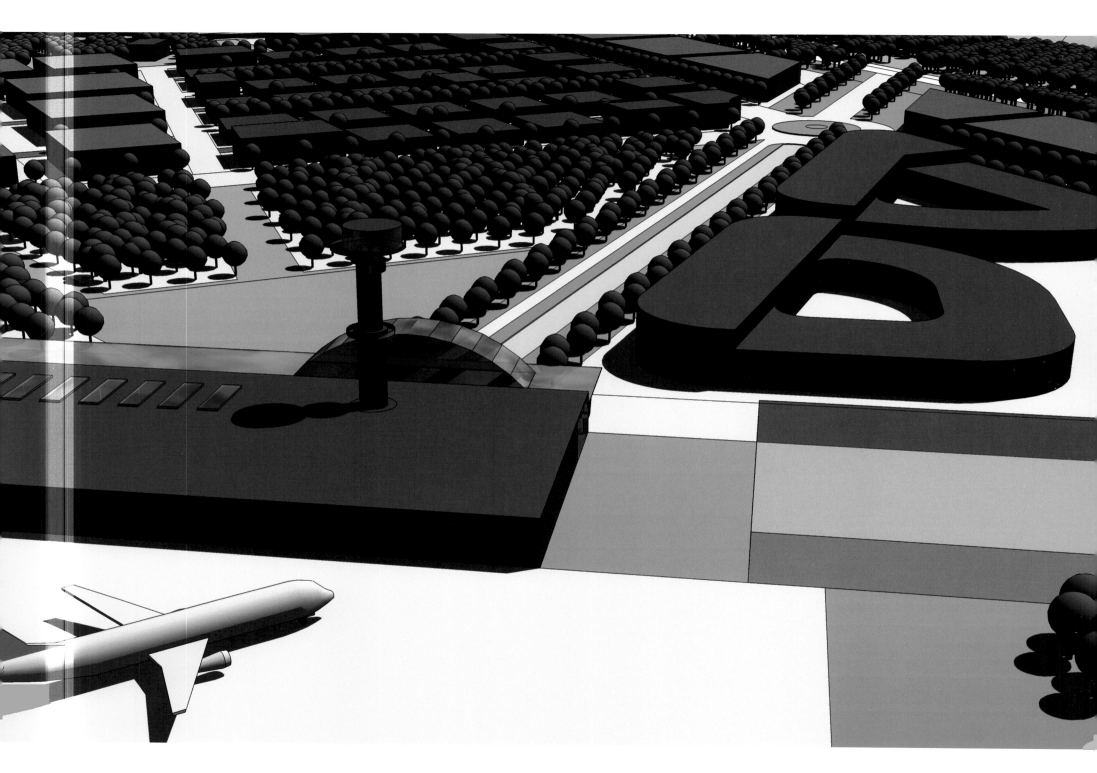

Enschede Airport Twente

DSOB ENSCHEDE
Johan Kok, Markus Götz, Franka Werner

The New City in the Old City

Roombeek and Twentse Welle
- Architecten Cie
- Sant & co
- DSOB Enschede
- SeARCH

Boddenkamp
- Rohmer
- Mulleners en Mulleners
- AWG

Zuiderval and Scholingsboulevard
- TKA
- DSOB Enschede
- IAA

Roombeek and Twentse Welle
Pi de Bruijn drew up the plan for the new Roombeek in intensive consultation with its inhabitants and the residents of adjacent areas. Edwin Santhagens and Marina Eenschoten designed the public space. The urban design is clear and logical. Lines from the surroundings and from the past have been carried through. The public space lives up to its name. The dwelling and building citizen contributes variation. In the spirit of the Oude Markt.
The former Roosendal industrial complex will house the new Twentse Welle museum, set to open in 2007. The factory was a genuine inspiration to architect Bjarne Mastenbroek. All its elements are still there – a footbridge, a water tower, saw-tooth roofs. They are complemented by elements from the architect's imagination and set in an entirely new arrangement. This creates a time machine. A glimpse of the past, the present and the future of a landscape under intense use for several millennia: Twente.

Boddenkamp

The same Lonneker railway line that has been transformed into a bus lane in Roombeek goes through Boddenkamp, which consists of an acacia grove, an old railway hangar and an abandoned bus depot within walking distance of the city centre and the Van Heekpark. The owners of the land, including the city, have formulated collective parameters that are intended to result in an attractive neighbourhood, urban living with the innovations alluded to in the introduction. Three architects have produced a preliminary design: Christine de Ruijter, Marlies Rohmer and Ton Mulleners. De Ruijter and Rohmer keep the bus lane on the route of the old railway line. They minimize its divisive effect by connecting it to a central open space. Mulleners adds a twist to the line and incorporates it in a section the breadth of the ring boulevard, right across the neighbourhood.

Zuiderval and Scholingsboulevard

Some of the big factory complexes in Enschede consisted of a series of buildings with the head end in or near the city centre and a body with its tail end linked to a railway line to the outside. Even when the textile industry was still operating, the clarity of this construction had already been obscured by diversification and redistribution. The Zuiderval is now the only place where this cohesion is being brought back, for a different purpose and in a different form.

A new approach road runs along the route of the former Zuiderspoorlijn ('southern railway') to Ahaus, linking the A35 motorway with the city centre. The road profile includes segregated cycle lanes and a new bus lane to the centre's two bus terminals. It is the main route to the Medisch Spectrum Twente (MST) medical centre, the largest non-academic hospital in the Netherlands and one of the few so centrally located within a city.

Offices, dwellings, a business centre and a large school for vocational training will be established along the Zuiderval. The Scholingsboulevard consists of two school buildings along an avenue perpendicular to the Zuiderval. The architect, Harry Abels, has come up with a striking shape that does justice both to generic and specific teaching activities. The school yard is a roof garden that provides a view of Enschede.

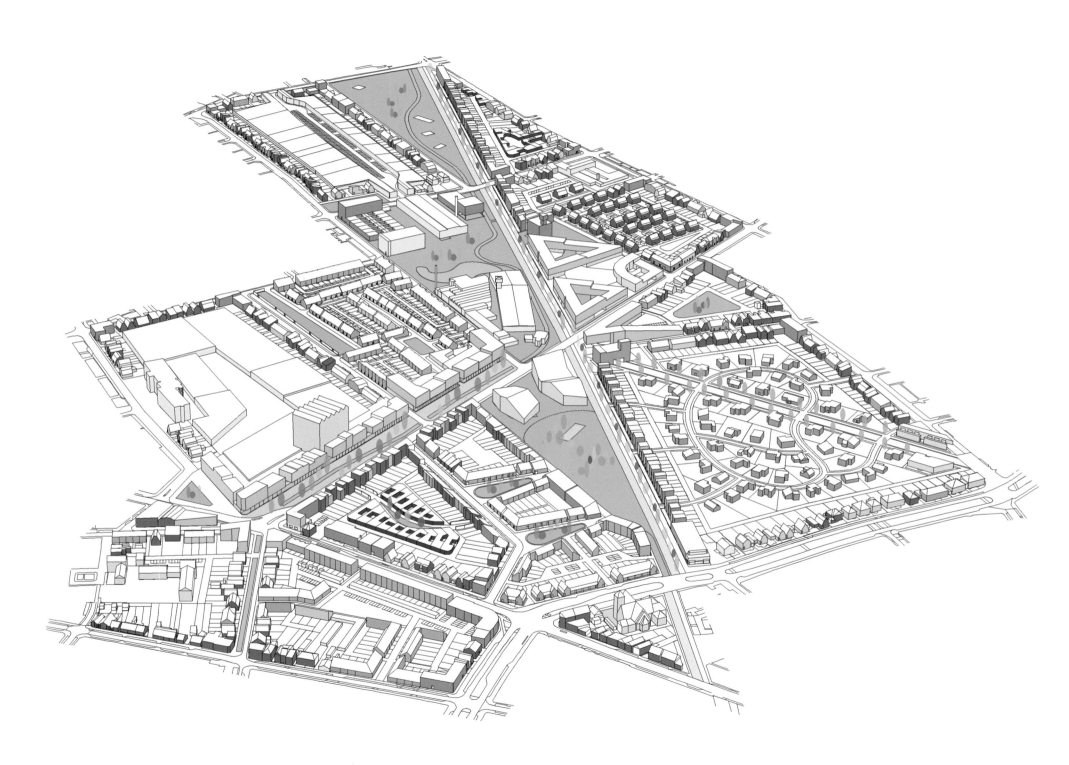

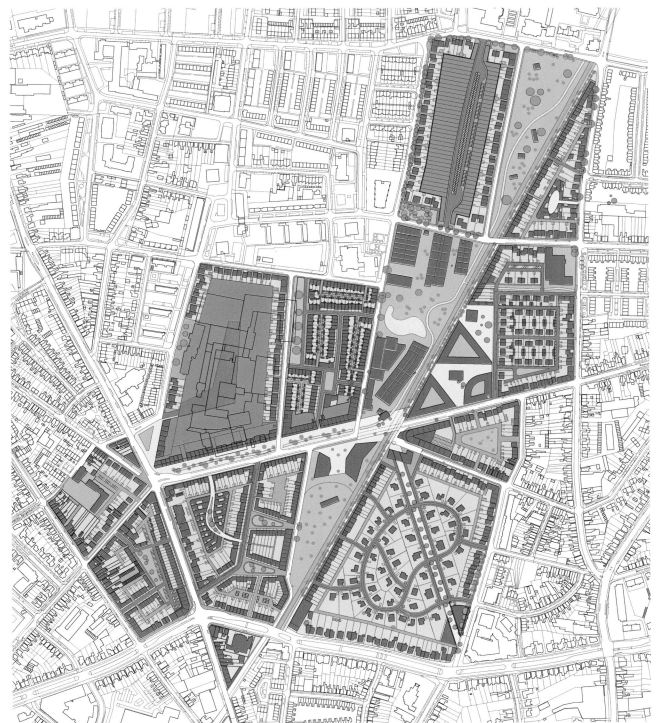

Roombeek - 1 - Urban Plan

ARCHITECTEN CIE
Pi de Bruijn, Joost van den Hoek

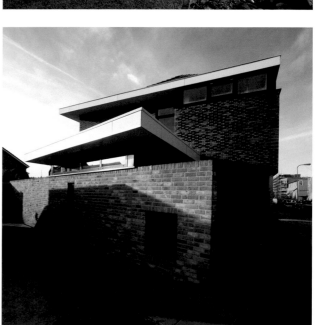

Photography Allard van der Hoek

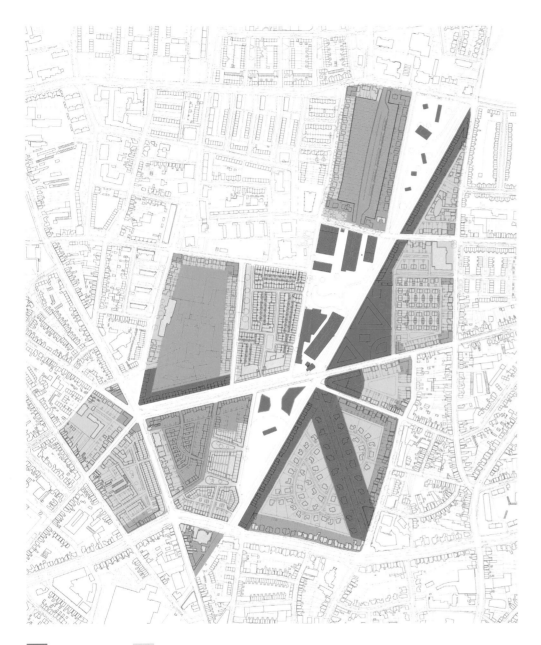

High   Low

Middle   Realized

Zoning plan

Roombeek - 2 - Private Patronage

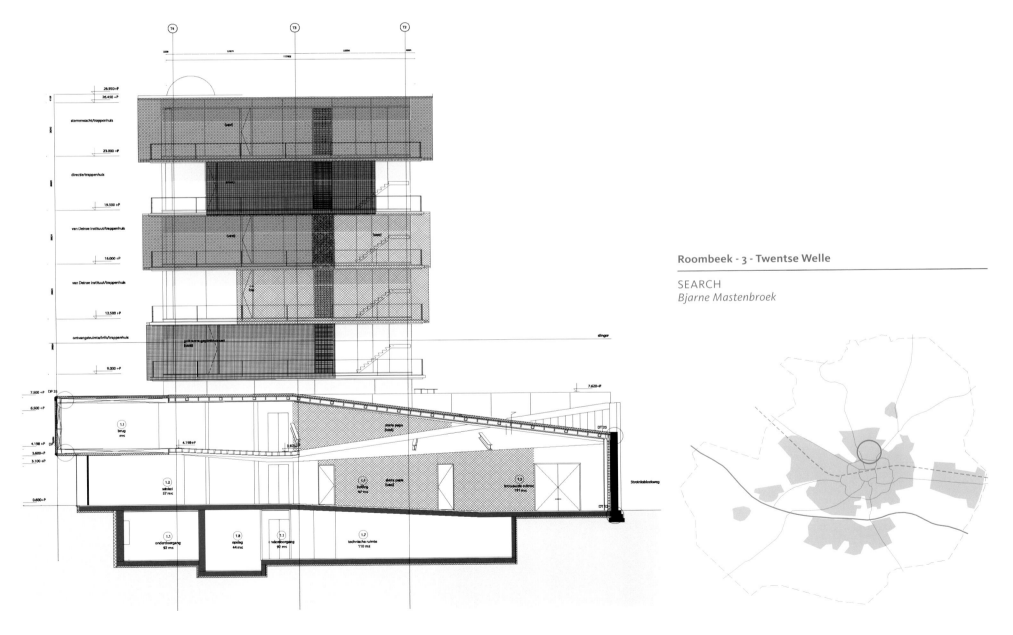

Roombeek - 3 - Twentse Welle

SEARCH
Bjarne Mastenbroek

ROHMER
Marlies Rohmer, Floris Hund

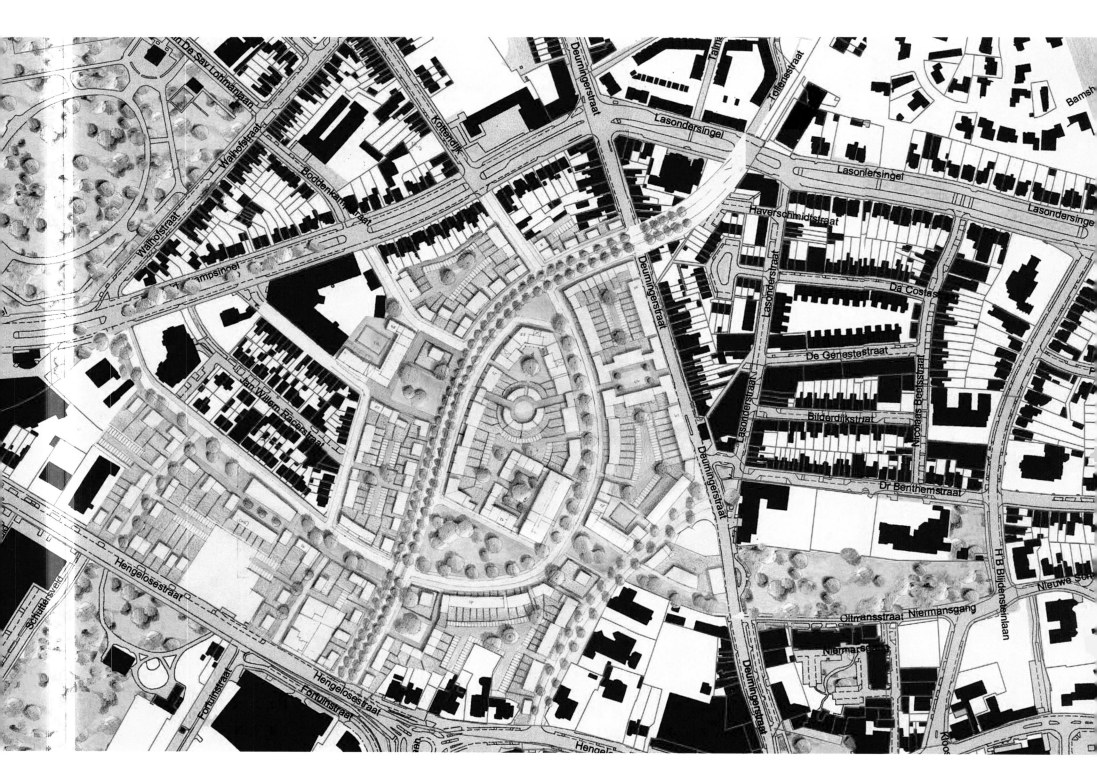

de nieuwe Boddenkamplaan: wonen in 3 lagen met kap

wonen in 2 of 3 lagen met kap

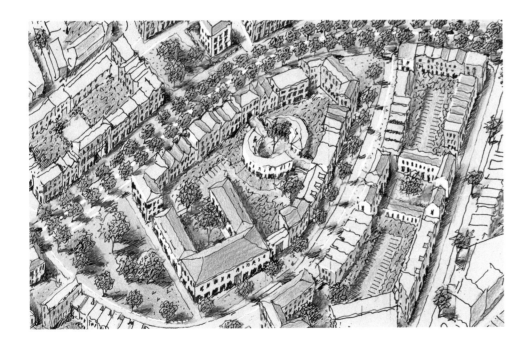

Boddenkamp - 2 -

MULLENERS & MULLENERS
Ton Mulleners

Boddenkamp - 3 -

AWG
Christine de Ruijter

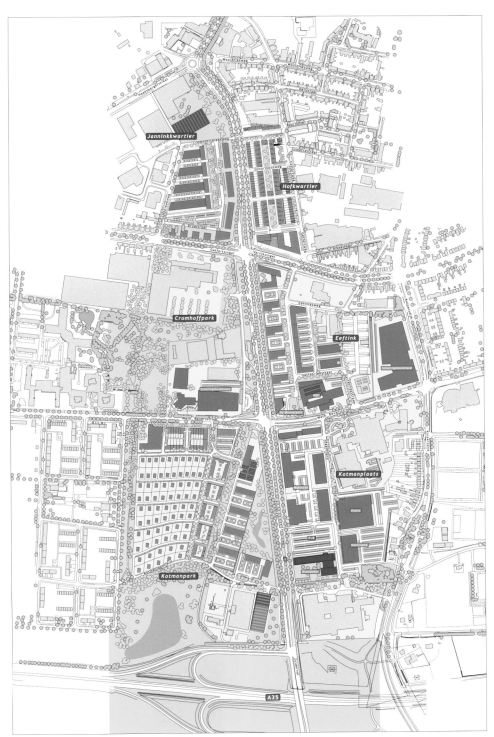

Zuiderval and Scholingsboulevard - 1 -

TKA/HANS DAVIDSON/DSOB ENSCHEDE
*TKA Teun Koolhaas/Hans Davidson/DSOB Enschede
David Diederix*

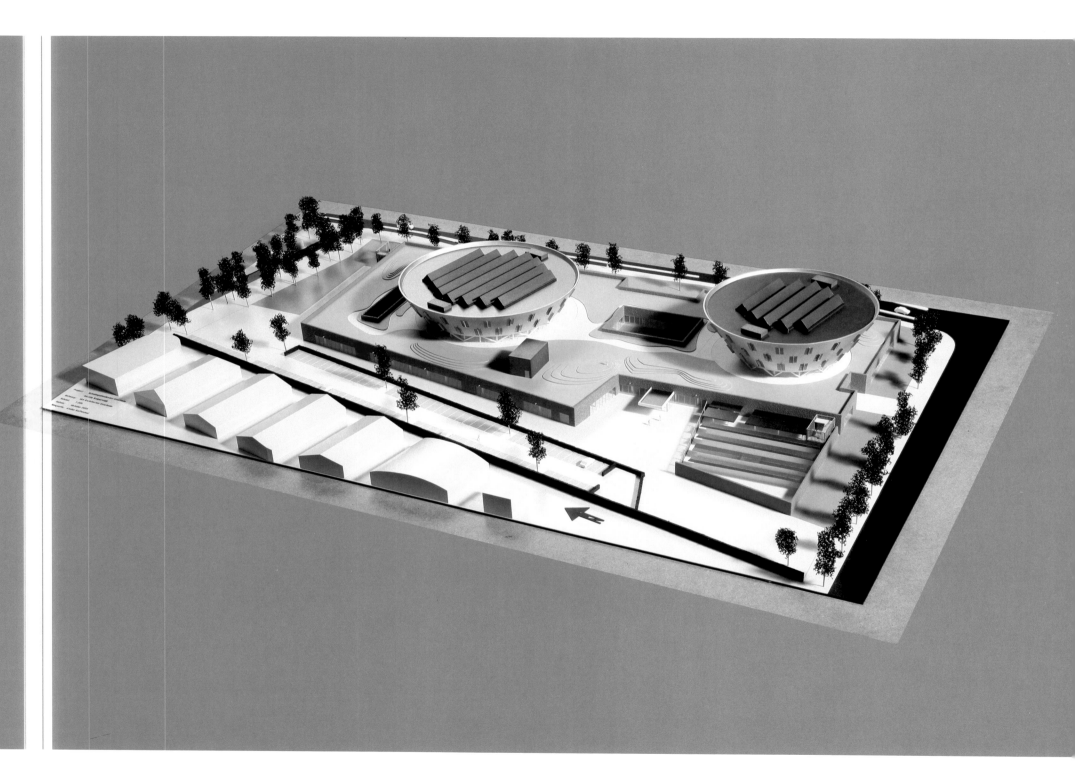

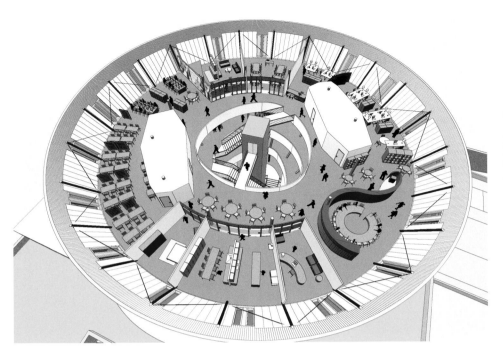

Zuiderval and Scholingsboulevard - 2 -

IAA ARCHITECTEN
Harry Abels

The Inner City

Railway Zone
- DSOB Enschede/IAA

Blijdensteinlaan 'Culture Ribbon'
- DSOB Enschede/Van der Jeugd Architecten

Europan
- Cornelisse/Verrijt

Wilmink Square/Station Square/Music Quarter
- DSOB Enschede
- Dick van Gameren/Onix Haiko
- MVRDV
- Zeinstra Van der Pol
- Ector Hoogstad

Klokkenplas and City Hall
- DSOB Enschede/IAA

Kop Boulevard/DISH/MST
- DSOB Enschede/IAA/ZZDP

Railway Zone

Many empty or extensively used sites in Enschede are located along the railway line. This has to do with the orientation of the vanished textile industry to the railway. Many of these areas are located within walking or cycling distance of the city centre and public transport hubs. An opportunity, therefore, for functions that are contingent on this. Car accessibility is already good; outside rush hour or against the direction of commuter traffic it's even excellent. Instead of adding buildings and functions, reinforcing the greenbelt structure with avenues and park areas or introducing new infrastructure like a cycle highway or parking garages is of course possible as well. The debate has only just begun.

The three studies in this book share the characteristic of the 'stained-glass principle': a continuous grid of public routes, streets, avenues, paths demarcates fields, each with its own colour. A second entrance to the station is also part of each plan. An extra entrance hall, ample facilities for driving up to the entrance, bicycle storage and a tunnel for pedestrians and cyclists on the north side of the railway line. The plaza on the south side of the station can then be closed to automobile traffic and become part of the *stadserf*.

Blijdensteinlaan 'Culture Ribbon'

The Rijksmuseum Twente's location was already somewhat eccentric, on the northern fringe of the ring. The establishment of the Twentse Welle, the AKI and the Cremer Institute in Roombeek will create a cluster of cultural functions north of the city. Time for a better connection. The Blijdensteinlaan is to become a promenade. Crossing the ring boulevard will be facilitated by the restoration of the central reservation at that point. The Rijksmuseum Twente will be surrounded by a sizable garden. There the promenade will link up with the Museumlaan, an avenue lined with four rows of trees, leading to the Cremer, the AKI and the Twentse Welle. In actual fact the distances are not very great. The new layout will make this apparent. The 'perceptual distance' will be shortened.

Europan

The European competition for young architects, Europan, has produced a balanced, circumspect and carefully elaborated plan for Enschede. Urban housing and employment on a currently more or less empty piece of land north of the city centre. When implemented, it will add – sticking with stained-glass terminology – a luminous field of deep, saturated colour in the grid of the railway zone.

Architects Floris Cornelisse and Robert Verrijt have designed a classic, in the line of De Bazel and Friedhoff: *'Calme, luxe et volupté'*. This *has* to be built. Preferably in Bentheimer sandstone. As a timeless enclave between the Boerenkerkhof and the modern elements of the city centre.

Wilmink Square/Station Square/Music Quarter

The ground plan for a new square is shaped like an hourglass. It will turn a disparate collection of buildings and remnant spaces between the railway line and Enschede's historic city centre into a single entity, part of the *stadserf*. The western section of the square, adjacent to the station, will be paved; the section for the new theatre building will be as green as the *gaarden* that were once located here, just outside the city walls. At its narrowest point, the square lies at the foot of a flight of stairs. This staircase leads to a hotel and an elevated music esplanade, the entrance to the music school. This is where the paved section of the square meets the green section. The focus of the square is the green copper dome designed by Hoogstad over the various halls and foyers of the new Music Theatre.

Upon entering the green section of the square, the church spire of the Grote Kerk and the tower of the City Hall are immediately visible, as well as the high-rises of the Molenstraat, behind the little tower of the Larinksticht convent. In the opposite direction, the western beginning and end points get the urban emphasis of a new tower in the space between the bus station plaza and the new station plaza.

Upon completion the two towers on the site of the fire station will also play a role in this perspective.

The station marks the beginning and end points on the west side; on the east side, situated 2 m higher, this is marked by the historic complex of the Larinksticht, with its garden, garden wall and tower. The complex will be extended with a new wing designed by Wytze Patijn.

The square will anchor Jan Hoogstad's building, home of the Dutch Touring Opera Company, theatre, pop music and music academy, in the city centre. On the south side a row of four buildings borders the square. Two of them are to be expanded or renovated, one is new and all of them are aligned with the fourth, the white nineteenth-century house with the rounded corner. On the north side, the extension to Frits van Dongen's Municipal Offices over the railway line and the hotel provide rear cover. The train will stop on the square like a tram. The platforms merge seamlessly with the *stadserf*.

Four combinations of clients and architects were invited to submit ideas for the functions, designs for the buildings and a bid for the land. All four plans are reproduced here. The choice fell on the design by Onix & Van Gameren, commissioned by Van Wijnen. It features a consistent and painstaking implementation of the plan. The contrast between the whimsical brick building to the south and the modernist hotel to the north of the 'suite doors', as the architects have dubbed the narrow part of the hourglass, as well as the clever use they make of Hoogstad's staircase, are additional qualities. They were the deciding factor.

Klokkenplas and City Hall

Close to the bustle of the Oude Markt and surrounded on all sides by shopping streets, the Klokkenplas is 'the eye of the storm'. A new arrangement and new functions will take advantage of this characteristic and make it visible.

A water garden inspired by the one in the Alhambra gives the space an atmosphere all its own. The Klokkenplas will become the City Hall's garden. The City Hall will be connected to the garden via the open doors of the future new public concourse. A new exhibition space for the Twente Architecture Centre, several new apartments and a restaurant with a terrace under the plane tree will shift the atmosphere from deserted to chic. The exhibition space makes use of existing cellars, which are connected to the garden via a patio. The water garden lies horizontal in the Klokkenplas, which slopes about 2 m up to the Oude Markt. One characteristic will make the other visible.

Top of the Boulevard/MST/Dish

If the MST can be linked to the inner city, Enschede's city centre will double in size. In order to achieve this, a pro-gramme must be added and the spaghetti of cycle paths, bus lanes, service roads and driveways that currently separate the two must be transformed into an attractive public space. The MST is larger than the inner city inside the historic city walls. Following the merger with the hospital on the Ariëns-plein, it has 1,000 beds. Twenty-five hundred people work there. Each day about 1,000 people come for a visit. The hospital wants to add an orientation to the inner city to the entrance on the Haaksbergerstraat, connected to a covered street inside the renovated building, the 'healthcare boul-evard'. A new lobby in a restored street façade of the Haaksbergerstraat, on the one hand, and an orientation to the city centre with a direct view of the City Hall tower, on the other, are linked in IAA's design by an ingenious system of patios, galleries and roof gardens. A city within the city, which facilitates the unavoidable changes in the layout of a major hospital.

A construction plan is in preparation for the Dish Hotel. A complete renovation and expansion of the hotel is combined with a block of flats. Residents of the blocks of flats can use the swimming pool and other facilities of the hotel.

To integrate the MST/Dish with the city centre, there is a proposal for a new city block on the site of the ING Bank and the vacant SLO Building. Sculptural volumes as high as 100 m provide a link to the zone of the former Boulevard 1945. The space between this block and the area containing the Dish Hotel and the Ten Hag Building will be laid out as a plaza, a variant of the bus plaza just a bit further east. The intersection of the former boulevard with the crucial link between the MST and the inner city is in the form of a roundabout. Bicycle and automobile traffic circle it, pedestrians have the shortest route. A large void links the underground spaces of the Van Heek garage with the *stadserf*.

DSOB ENSCHEDE/IAA ARCHITECTEN
DSOB Enschede Ton Schaap, Franka Werner, Wim Salomons/
IAA Architecten Rick Bruggink

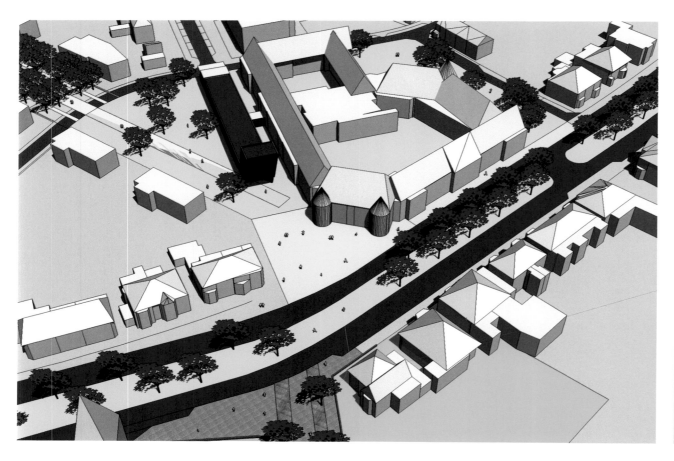

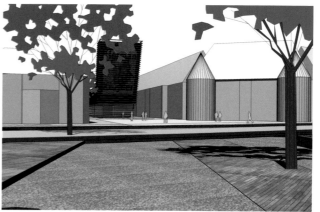

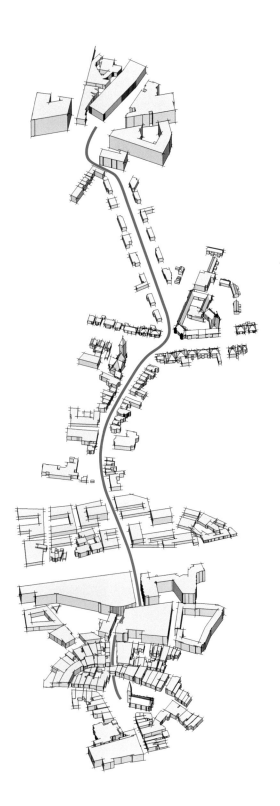

Blijdensteinlaan 'Culture Ribbon'

DSOB ENSCHEDE/VAN DER JEUGD ARCHITECTEN
DSOB Enschede Marina Eenschoten, Hans Schröder/
Van der Jeugd Architecten Paul van der Jeugd

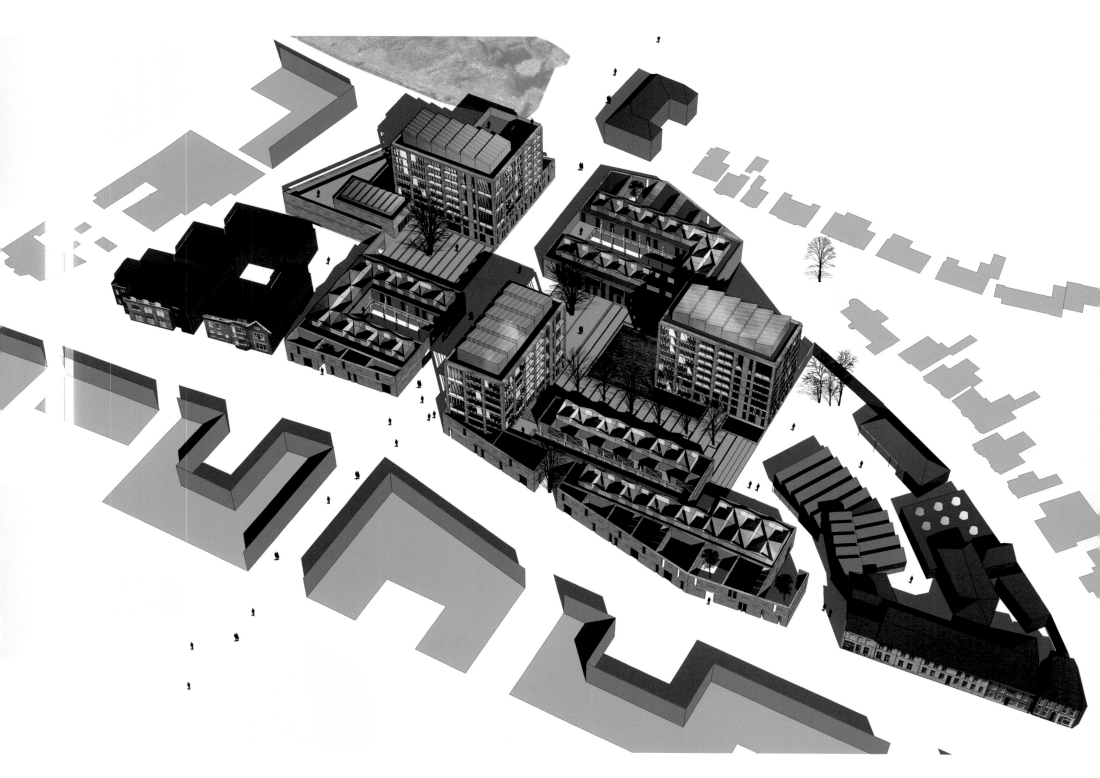

Europan

CORNELISSE/VERRIJT
Floris Cornelisse, Robert Verrijt

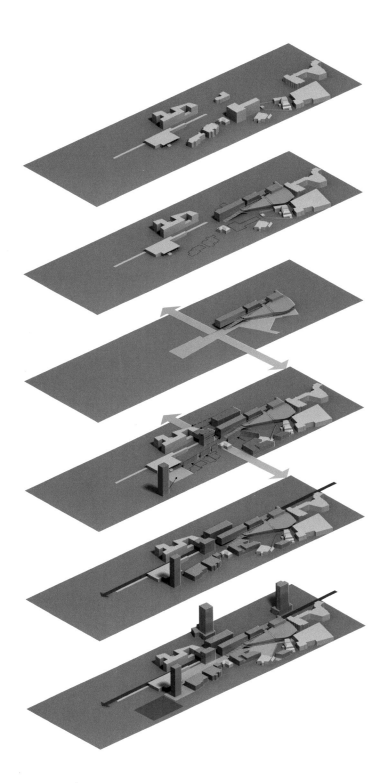

Wilmink Square/Station Square/Music Quarter - 1 -

DSOB ENSCHEDE
Ton Schaap, Franka Werner

Wilmink Square/Station Square/Music Quarter - 2 -

DICK VAN GAMEREN/ONIX
Dick van Gameren/ONIX Haiko Meijer

Wilmink Square/Station Square/Music Quarter - 3

MVRDV
Nathalie de Vries

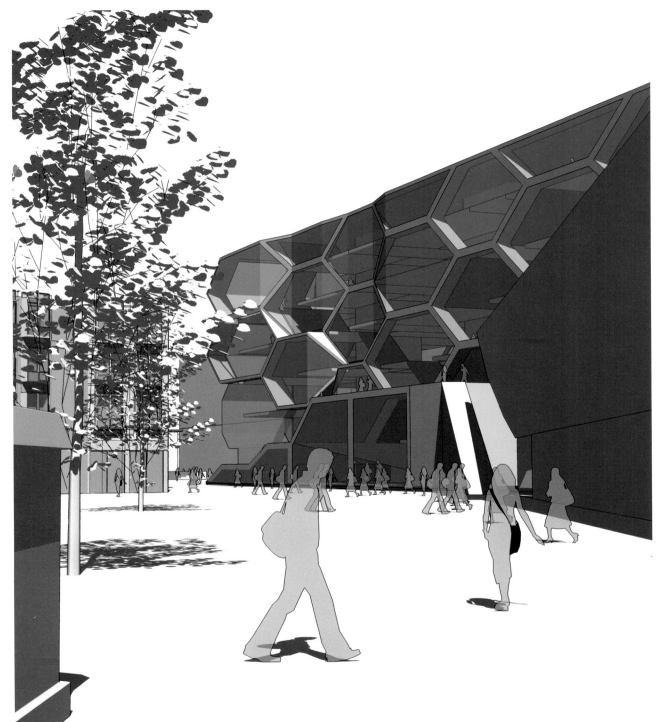

Wilmink Square/Station Square/Music Quarter - 4 -

ZEINSTRAVANDERPOL
Liesbeth van der Pol

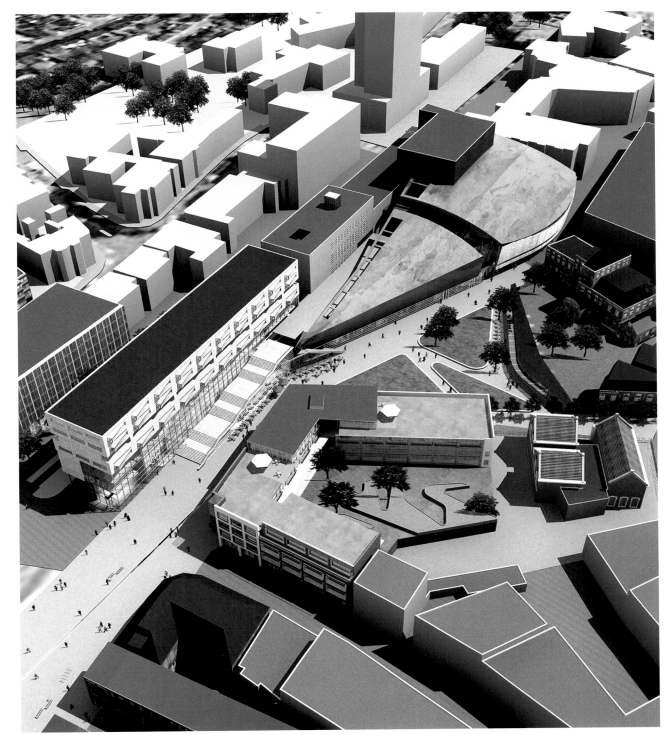

Wilmink Square/Station Square/Music Quarter - 5 -

ECTOR HOOGSTAD
Joost Ector, Jan Hoogstad

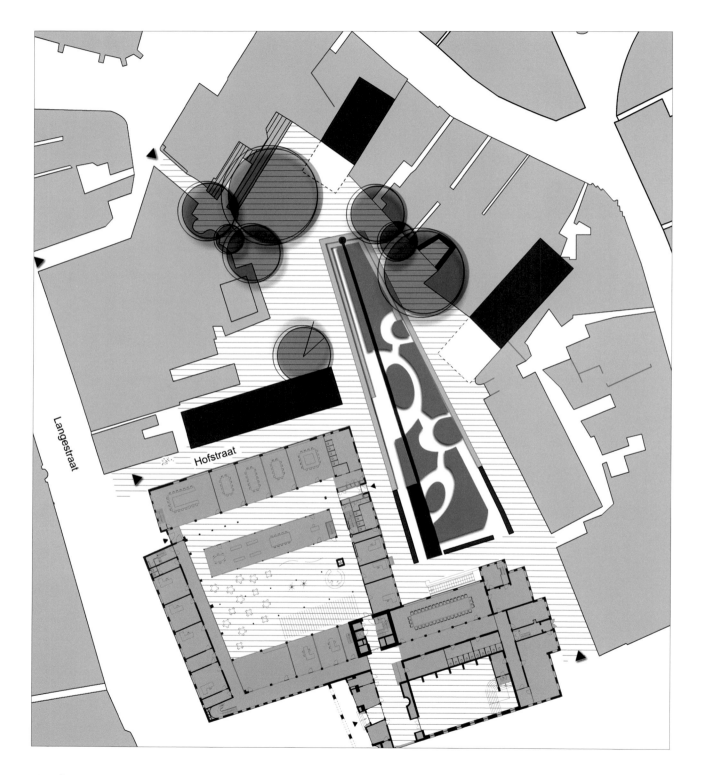

Langestraat

Hofstraat

Klokkenplas and City Hall

DSOB ENSCHEDE/IAA ARCHITECTEN
DSOB Enschede Hans Schröder/IAA Architecten Harry Abels

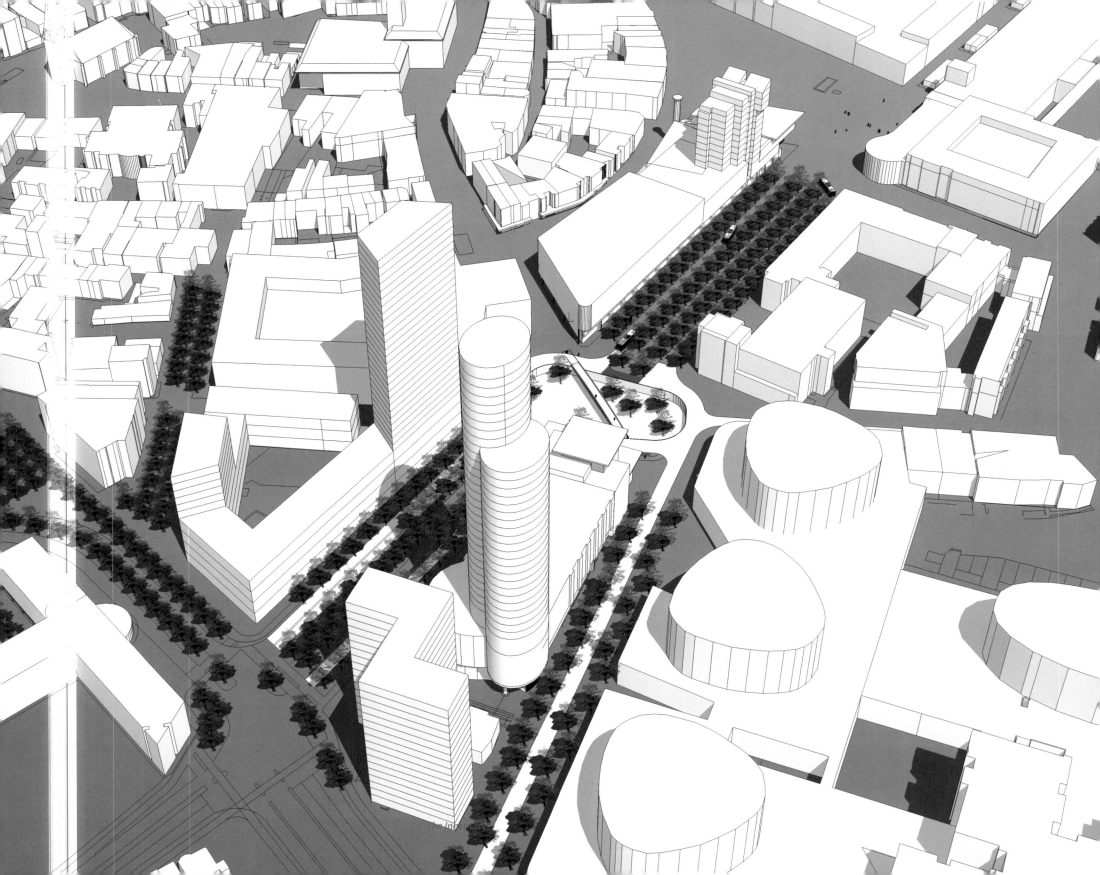

Top of the Boulevard/MST/Dish - 1 -

DSOB ENSCHEDE/IAA ARCHITECTEN/ZZDP
*DSOB Ton Schaap, David Diederix, Wim Salomons/
IAA Architecten Harry Abels/ZZDP Joris Deur,
Maarten Groeneveld, Nesja Zahtila*

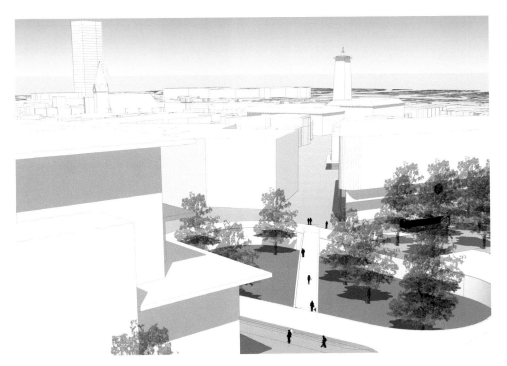

Top of the Boulevard/MST/Dish - 2 -

ZZDP
Maarten Groeneveld, Nesja Zahtila

Photography Locations